WELCOME PLANET EARTH

Hold on tight!

Hello. I'm Nav the alien and I hope you enjoy *Welcome to Planet Earth*. This edition of *The Navigator* is all about your lovely planet and how you humans get around it. On your journey through these pages, you'll find out lots of interesting facts about things above and below you; about things on land and in the water; and about fascinating people and places – both past and present. You'll come across tornadoes, volcanoes, Romans, Vikings, dolphins and amazing plants ... phew!

Let the journey begin!

ext Type	Literacy Skills	Wider Curriculum Links
count/Report	Skimming and scanning; close reading; deductive comprehension; linking information	**Geography** Unit 7: Weather around the world
port	Locating information; reading for information; making selections; justifying opinions	**History** Unit 6A: Why have people invaded and settled in Britain in the past?
port	Locating information; reading for information; making selections; justifying	**History** Unit 6A: Why have people invaded and settled in Britain in the past?
port (visual)	Interpreting visuals	**Science** Unit 3D: Rocks and soils
ference	Close reading of visual information; making links between text and visuals; justifying options	**Geography** Unit 24: Passport to the world
port	Skimming and scanning; locating information	**Science** Unit 3B: Helping plants grow well
count	Locating information; comparing information; deductive and inferential comprehension	**Art and Design** Unit 3C: Can we change places?
tters: count	Skimming and scanning; deductive and inferential comprehension	
ference	Vocabulary development; using a reference text; skimming and scanning	**History** Unit 6C: Why have people invaded and settled in Britain in the past?
port	Skimming and scanning; close reading; deductive and inferential comprehension	**Geography** Unit 7: Weather around the world
n spread		
		ICT: Year 3 Schemes of work

Howard Bluestein is a storm chaser. When most people hear that hurricane or a tornado is about to strike, they get as far away as they can. Not Howard Bluestein! As soon as he hears a report of a storm, he jumps into his van and tries to follow i Bluestein is excited by the power of storms, but he is also a scientist. He chases tornadoes to find out more about them. A tornado is a moving column of fast-spinning air. Information such as air pressure and wind speed helps scientists to understanc tornadoes better and to predict when they might strike.

STORM
chaser

WAITING. . .

Many tornadoes occur in a large area in the United States called Tornado Alley. This is where Bluestein spends his days in spring and early summer – tornado season! Bluestein and his team drive a van equipped with radar. While they drive, Bluestein listens to weather reports on the radio. If they think a storm might produce a tornado, they chase it.

A TORNADO STRIKES!

One day in 1995, for example, Bluestein suddenly noticed dust swirling below a huge, black thunder cloud. Soon a long, thin funnel reached from the ground into the thunder cloud – a tornado! The radar showed winds of 200 kilometres per hour moving towards them.

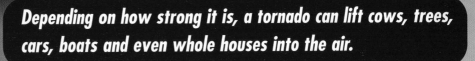

AFTER THE STORM

When it was over, the storm chasers drove to the area where the tornado had been. What a sight! Electric poles lay flat on the ground, a farm had lost its roof, and several cows lay dead in a field. Luckily, the local people had hidden in a special storm shelter and so they were all safe. When Bluestein saw the damage, he knew the radar measurements were right. This had been a very strong tornado!

MEASURING TORNADOES

The faster a tornado spins, the more damage it can cause. This table shows what can happen as the speed of a tornado increases. The tornado Bluestein watched in 1995 was a Level 2.

Level	Wind speed	Damage
0	64–116 kph	Branches broken off trees
1	117–180 kph	Caravans overturned; cars pushed off roads
2	181–253 kph	Large trees uprooted; roofs torn off homes; caravans destroyed; light objects fly about
3	254–332 kph	Forests uprooted; trains overturned; walls and roofs damaged
4	333–419 kph	Houses flattened; cars thrown; large objects fly about
5	420–512 kph	Strong houses lifted into air; cars flung through air

The Rough Guide to ROME

Just 1000 years ago, Rome was a village. Today it is the capital of the Roman Empire and one of the greatest cities in the world. Rome is a perfect place to visit. It has big open squares and beautiful buildings, and there are many things to see and do.

THE THEATRE

Open All day **Price** Free

This theatre is so big that the actors wear masks – it's the only way to see them from the back. Seats up to 10 000. Snacks and drinks for sale.

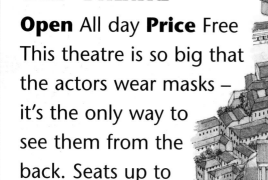

THE FORUM   **Open** All day and night   **Price** Free

A huge open square where Romans like to shop, make money, visit a temple and catch up with all the news. The Forum contains many important buildings. The most beautiful is the Temple of Vesta with its tall white columns, mosaic floors and cool, shady garden.

EXPLORING ROME

Rome's 'must-see' places are in the city centre on the right bank of the River Tiber.

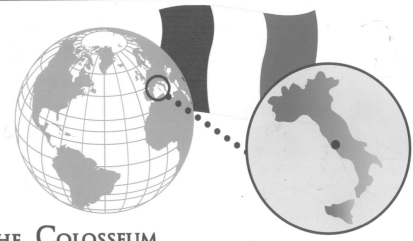

THE COLOSSEUM

Open Sunrise to sunset   **Price** Free

A huge open-air arena that holds exciting fights between gladiators, animals and slaves. These shows are not for everyone: the seats are hard, the sun is hot and there can be a lot of blood. But it's a good place to spot the Emperor! Seats up to 50 000. Snacks and drinks for sale.

THE CIRCUS

Open Every afternoon **Price** 1 bronze coin

Romans love chariot-racing and this is the largest race track in the city. Buy a ticket, choose one of the four teams (red, green, blue or white) and shout along with the crowd. Seats up to 300 000. Snacks and drinks for sale.

Planning your Trip

GETTING AROUND The best way [to] get around Rome is on foot, although [the] streets can be muddy and very busy. Remember that the city is built on seve[n] hills, so bring a comfortable pair of sho[es].

WHEN TO VISIT Rome is very hot in the summer. In the spring [and] autumn the days are warm and bright, but there may be rain showe[rs]. In winter, the weather is cool, but there are fewer tourists.

SHOPPING

It's fun to shop in Rome. There are many kinds of shops in the city's streets and all sorts of stalls in the markets. The best buys are cloth, shoes, olive oil and dates.

Trajan's Market

The city's biggest market is near the Forum. It has over 150 shops selling everything from silver to wine. Look out for the **slave market** where the Romans buy their slaves.

Marcus's Cloth Shop, Via Ostia

The richest Romans get their togas here. Why not buy one as a souvenir?

BED AND BATH The best place to stay is in a tavern near the Forum. Be sure to ask for a room at the back. The streets are full of carts at night and can be very noisy. Try to visit the Public Baths. This is where Romans go to soak in the hot and cold baths, and to read, exercise, meet their friends, have a massage and play a game of dice. The prices are cheap and children go free.

EATING OUT Romans enjoy their food. You will find all sorts of places to enjoy a meal. Some of them are expensive, but most are very cheap.

Julia's Tavern, Via Luca	House of Flora, Via Maria	Julius the Baker, Via Roma
Sells hot take-away food. Good, spicy dishes such as cabbage with leeks.	A busy tavern selling stuffed dormice and other Roman dishes.	Bakes honey cakes and fresh bread twice a day.

WHEN IN ROME Everyone in Rome speaks Latin. Try your best to speak a few words. The Romans really like it!

ENGLISH	LATIN
Hello	Salve! (*sal-way*)
Goodbye	Vale! (*wal-ay*)
How much?	Quantum (*kwontum*)
Where?	Ubi (*oobi*)
Yes	Ita (*ittah*)
No	Non (*nown – to rhyme with 'bone'*)
Please	Sis (*seess*)
Thank you	Bene facis (*ben-eh fass-is*)

The distance from the ground beneath your feet to the centre of the Earth is about 6500 kilometres. That's quite a way! People go deep underground in tunnels, caves and mines, but no one has been anywhere near the Earth's centre. The deepest anyone has descended underground is just 3.5 km, in a diamond mine. If you imagine the Earth as an apple, 3.5 km does not even break through the skin.

This diagram shows the Earth's layers. Although we cannot travel deep into the Earth, scientists called geologists have worked out what is there by studying earthquakes and volcanoes.

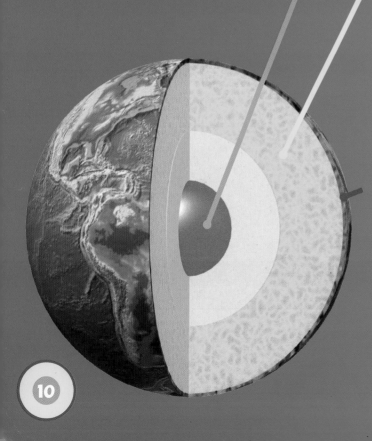

CORE The core is the Earth's centre. It is made up of two layers. The inner core is a ball of hot solid metal. The outer core is a layer of hot liquid metal.

MANTLE The mantle lies between the core and the crust. It is made up of hot rock. In fact, in some places the rock is so hot it melts. The molten rock is called magma.

CRUST The outer layer of the Earth is called the crust. This is a layer of solid rock between 6 and 70 kilometres thick. The crust is thinnest where it stretches under the oceans and thickest where it rises up to make the continents.

VOLCANO

...upts through a
...eak spot in the
...rth's crust. When
...agma flows out
...a volcano, it is
...led lava.

250 m – *deepest road and rail tunnels*

1 km – *deepest coal mines*

1.5 km – *deepest explored cave*

3.5 km – *deepest diamond mines*

11 km – *deepest oil well*
11 km – *deepest submarine dive*

13 km – *deepest borehole*

This cross section shows some of the greatest depths reached under the ground and in the oceans.

LEGOLAND HERE I COME!

Kezia and her grown-up sister are going to Legoland. They onl[y] have half a day. Kezia knows ju[st] which rides she wants to go on.

WAVE SURFER

MY TOWN

TECHNIC GARAGE

COCA-COLA FOUNTAIN

MY TOWN HARBOUR AND SHOW

BRICK BROTHERS SOUVENIR CO.

MAGIC THEATRE

BRICKADILLY'S CAROUSEL, CHAIROPLANE & FERRIS WHEEL

THE EXPLORER'S INSTITUTE

I-SPY EXPRESS

BOATING SCHOOL

DRIVING SCHOOL VAUXHALL

LEGO TRAFFIC

PIZZA PERGOLA

THE HILL TR[AIN]

BALLOON SCHOOL

DRIVERS

PASTA PATCH

THE HARE & THE TORTOISE WILLOW STAGE JACK & THE BEANSTALK

FAIRY TALE BROOK

duplo TRAIN

LEGO Clothes 'n' Stuff

WATER WORKS

Whirly Birds

MINILAND

duplo PLAYTOWN

duplo GARDENS

CHALLENGE

THE BUILDING SITE

DACTA WORKSHOPS

TRELSTYLE WORKSHOPS

PAPA MOLE'S

MANSION HOUSE

HOSPITALITY VENUE LEGOLAND

LEGOLAND

SKY RIDER

IMAGINATION THEATRE

NEW FOR 2001 LEGO LIFE ON MARS

TH[E] HILL

IMAGINATION CENTRE

12

Can you help her decide in which order to visit them? Check the **Ride Safety Guide** to make sure that Kezia can go on the rides she has chosen. She is 1.0m tall. Remember, Kezia and her sister will want to eat during their visit, too!

RIDE SAFETY GUIDE

To ride, children must be at least:

A 0.9m tall   **B** 1.0m tall   **C** 1.1m tall

D Children at least 1.0m to be accompanied by an adult

E Children at least 1.1m to be accompanied by an adult

Beware — you will get wet!

Things I want to see and do

* Magic theatre
* Miniland
* Balloon school
* Boating school
* Waterworks
* The Hill Train
* Wave Surfer
* Food!

Plant Survivors

All plants need water and sunlight to grow and live. But some plants can survive in the strangest places ...

Hitchhiker plants

Epiphytes are plants that hitchhike a ride on other plants to reach sunlight. They climb up by twisting their stems around taller plants or trees. Some epiphytes send out long roots to absorb water from the air, or to reach down to streams far below to keep them alive during dry spells.

This epiphyte is called a bromeliad. Its long, dangling roots can grow up to 18 metres long.

Snow-busters

Some plants, such as gentians, mountain pinks and saxifrages, grow on cold, high mountains. They save energy by growing very slowly. It can take them a whole year to grow two tiny leaves.

Like many plants, the alpine snowbell disappears underground during the winter. When new shoots start to push up through the snow in spring, they give off enough heat to melt the snow around them.

Cacti have spines rather than leaves. These spines help to protect the plant from the heat of the desert.

Desert plants

Desert plants survive on very little water. Cacti store rainwater in their fleshy stems. The creosote bush sends out huge networks of roots so it can seek out every drop of dew or rain. Some seeds lie waiting for rain. They burst into life when rain falls, then flower, set seed and die — all in a few days.

Fire-beaters

Some plants can grow even when fires have destroyed their habitats. Red oat grass has a seed which can burrow down below burnt earth. The seed has a long tail which twists in the hot soil, helping the seed to spiral its way underground.

All of these plants have found amazing ways to survive the odds.

WHO WAS HENRY MOORE?

Henry Moore was one of the most important artists of the twentieth century. He made huge sculptures out of stone, wood and bronze. Read on to find out more about Henry's life, and to see some of his amazing sculptures and drawings.

CASTLEFORD SCHOOL ROLL OF HONOUR

Henry's teachers recognised that he was a talented artist. When he was sixteen, he was asked to carve this roll of honour for his school. It listed the names of former pupils who were going off to fight in World War I.

THE WEST WIND

Henry made this sculpture for the London Underground. He was interested in different ways of representing wind, fire and water. In this sculpture he represents the wind as a powerful woman.

A SCULPTOR'S LIFE

1898	1910	1917	1921
Born on 30 July in Castleford, Yorkshire	Went to Castleford Grammar School	Fought in World War I for two years	Joined the Royal College of Art in London

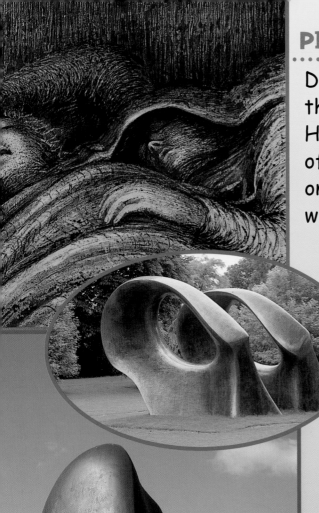

PINK AND GREEN SLEEPERS

During World War II, Henry drew the daily life of people in London. Henry's war drawings were some of his most powerful works. This one shows people trying to sleep while bombs exploded outside.

DOUBLE OVAL

In the 1950s and 60s, Henry started to make huge sculptures from bronze and wood, as well as from stone. He wanted people to look at his sculptures from all sides. As you walk around this sculpture, you see different views through the two holes.

SHEEP PIECE

Through the window of his studio, Henry could see sheep grazing. In 1971, he made this abstract sculpture of the sheep. It still stands in the field outside his studio.

17

GREETINGS MOTHER

As you know, I would rather have gone to Xygggl for my summer holidays, but Earth has turned out to be quite an interesting planet. You won't believe it, but people even travel in boxes. Yes, really! Whereas we move from place to place in sensible bubbles, these primitive Earth people get about by many strange means.
For example . . .

They crowd together in sheds with windows. The sheds are all joined together and zoom along long, thin rails. Once they are in these moving sheds, the people hardly ever talk to one another. They put headphones on and listen to things in private, or speak to small flat boxes in their hands, and look at things called 'papers' and 'books'.

Sometimes they climb up steps into enormous cylinders with wings and sit as close together as they can, while the cylinders fly them to far-off beaches. There the people lie quite still for a week or two with hardly anything on. Then they climb back into the winged cylinders and go home again, wearing stupid hats and looking unhappy.

here is one particular type of small travelling box that is
absolutely everywhere. Underneath they have four round things
called wheels. These boxes travel at speed for some time, then
join long lines of other boxes and move very, very slowly for
miles. I don't understand this at all.

Another popular Earth vehicle has just two wheels and can
carry only one or two people at a time. They are propelled
by the driver's feet, which go round and round quite fast.
The drivers wear special helmets in case they fall off and
hurt themselves.

Well, I must go now, Mother. I'm about to enter the
flying teacup that will take me home to our lovely
green skies, our beautiful underground houses,
and our very sensible travel bubbles.

See you soon.
Your loving son,
Kwllzyzzzukkybott

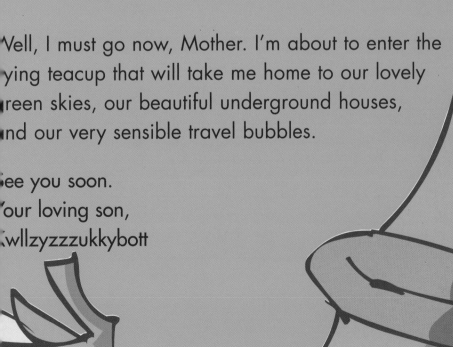

Have you ever wondered where words come from?
Why do we call a hole filled with glass a 'window'?
Why is the space above us called the 'sky'?

crook

1. *a bend, curve or twist*
2. *someone who is dishonest*

From the word 'krokr', meaning *hook, peg, curve, bend, winding* or *corner*. Originally, the word meant something that was bent or curved like a shepherd's crook or a peg, but it later came to mean someone who is dishonest.

In Australia, 'crook' also means 'unwell'. Perhaps it comes from the idea of an ill person being 'bent over' with pain!

leg

1. *the part of the body that an animal or human stands on*
2. *a pole or post supporting a table or chair*

From the word 'leggr', meaning *thigh*. The word that was used before this was 'shank'.

The phrase 'travelling on Shank's pon means walking.

sky

the space we see above us whe we are outside.
From the word 'sky', which actually means *cloud*!

WORDS

The English language has been influenced over the years by the people who have invaded and settled in Britain. The Vikings for example, added many more new words to the language. Here are some of the words they gave us:

take

to catch, to seize, to capture
From the word 'taka', meaning to grasp, seize or catch. There are many ways in which we use this word. We can take a bus, a photograph or a holiday. We can take our PE kit to school, or someone in a car. We can take after our parents, take away fish and chips, take in the view, take off our clothes, take over a company, take turns to throw the die, take up jogging. Events can take place. 'Take' can also mean 'steal'.

troll

small, mythological creature
The word 'troll' in Scandinavian myths originally meant giant, but has come to mean a dwarf or an imp.

want

1. to have a desire for
2. to be without something
From the word 'wanta', meaning to be lacking, to be without.

window

an opening in a building or vehicle, to let in light and air
From two words 'vind' + 'auga', meaning wind-eye. Before the Vikings came, the word for window was 'eagdura', meaning eye-door.

When photography was first introduced, many people were suspicious of the camera. They felt that part of themselves had been taken away, or stolen, every time they were photographed.

THE BEST REWARD EVER

Have you ever wondered what it would be like to swim with dolphins? Some children actually get the chance ... Dr Nathanson works in America with children who have special needs. He helps them to learn how to pay attention and follow instructions. He knew from his work that children often tried harder if they knew that they would get a reward. He thought that, for some children, playing or swimming with dolphins would be the best reward ever. In 1989, Dr Nathanson set up a therapy programme in Florida and called it Dolphin Human Therapy.

WHY DOLPHINS?

Dolphins are clever animals and like being around people. They 'talk' to each other and try hard to find ways to communicate with people. The dolphins that work in Dr Nathanson's centre are gentle and calm and seem to know straight away how to act with the children.

1 First, trainers help the child to get used to the feel of their swimming partner in the water. Dolphins can be slippery!

HOW DOES IT WORK?
If the child tries hard to do what Dr Nathanson and his assistant ask, they get to play or swim with a dolphin as a reward.

2 Next, trainers swim alongside the child as the dolphin swims. The dolphin swims on its back, so the child can hold onto its fins.

3 Soon, the dolphin and rider are off for a swim around the pool!

ESSENTIAL FACTS

● Children from 50 countries have been helped by Dolphin Human Therapy.

● Each child has his or her own special treatment plan.

● Dr Nathanson and his team have carried out more than 20 000 treatment sessions.

23

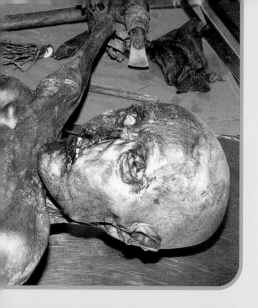

Ancient Backpacker

In 1991, the mummified remains of a man were found in the Alps. He became known as 'the Iceman'. This Stone Age traveller had set out on a journey that would last 5000 years. Experts think that he may have been running away from his village when he fell over and was buried by the snow. He was carrying a back pack made from tree bark and branches.

Worldwide travel is becoming quicker and easier all the time. Today we can travel all the way around the world in 24 hours. But that's nothing compared to these incredible journeys!

THE HITCH GUIDE TO

Speeding Butterflies

In North America, swarms of Monarch butterflies migrate south in the autumn to spend the winter months in Mexico. They can fly nearly 2000 kilometres in a few days, and reach speeds around 50 kilometres an hour in still air. In the spring, they begin the long journey home again.

Plague of Rabbits

Rabbits were first taken to Australia in 1788 on ships carrying convicts from Britain. The journey of more than 24000 kilometres took around eight months. Rabbits only became established in the wild in 1859, after a small group was released for people to hunt. Within 20 years, millions of them had devastated the land. In 1948, a virus called myxomatosis was introduced, which helped to reduce the number of rabbits.

Today we buy car stickers and T-shirts to show where we have been on our travels. In the Middle Ages, pilgrims tied scallop shells to their clothing to show that they were on a pilgrimage.

HIKER'S THE PLANET

Homesick Salmon

Pacific salmon spend their whole lives travelling. After hatching in freshwater rivers and streams, they spend up to four years at sea before they return to their home rivers to breed. They travel hundreds of kilometres, leaping up steep waterfalls and dodging strong currents. They know when they have arrived, because they remember the exact mix of minerals, plants and animals in their home waters.

Byte-Sized ICT

ICT: Unit 3a

Word-processing; changing fonts

Greetings mother!

Greetings again, mother!

Fancy being an alien for a while? The alien, Xwllzyzzzukkybott, wrote a g-mail (on pages 18 and 19) to his mother all about life on Earth. He told her what he thought of the transport we use on Earth.

Imagine you are Xwllzyzzzukkybott and are typing a second g-mail to your mother. This time you could tell her what you think about something else on this weird planet, Earth. How about telling her about the strange homes people live in? Or maybe you've just tried Earth food. What would you think of that? How would you describe it to your mother?

See if you can find a font suitable for an alien!

Storm chaser

Web weather watch

Can you find out about an interesting, unusual or disastrous weather event? There are lots of useful websites which give information about the weather. Using a search engine site will help you find them.

Here are some questions to help you:

- *What kind of weather did it involve?*
- *What happened?*
- *Where did it happen?*
- *Was there any damage?*
- *Do scientists know why it happened?*

What's underneath?

Volcano picture

ICT: Unit 3a

Combining text and graphics

Why not have a go at using an art package to draw a diagram of a volcano? You might need to find out a bit more about volcanoes first, perhaps using a CD-ROM encyclopedia.

Make your diagram a cross-section, like the cross section diagram of the Earth on pages 10 and 11. This means it looks as if you have sliced through the volcano. Use different colours to show the layers and add some labels using the 'text' button.

The Rough Guide to Rome

Roman baths research challenge

Can you find out some more information about Roman baths? Use a CD-ROM or the Internet to find out what the different kinds of baths were called and some of the things a Roman would do there.

Romans also had an interesting way of removing the dirt from their skin. Can you find how they did it?

Who was Henry Moore?

Digital sculptures

Are you a budding sculptor? Have a go at creating a mini sculpture from whatever materials you have around. How about making one of an animal using modelling clay, or you could try to represent wind, fire or water, just like Henry Moore did. Make it look different from each side.

When you have finished, take some digital photographs showing your sculpture from different sides. You could even take one looking down on your sculpture. Arrange the photos on one page to show all the views. Give your sculpture a name and include that on your page.

Plant survivors

Survival notes

The plants on pages 14 and 15 are amazing, aren't they? Why not make up a quiz about them for a friend. Start by refreshing your memory and re-reading the page.

It might be helpful to type some very brief notes in a word processor. First type the name of the each plant in bold. Then underneath, type one or two key words to remind you where it lives and what is special or unusual about it. Print out your notes and quiz your friend about the plants and their strange behaviour. If you have time, you could type out your questions first. If you prefer, you could work with a partner to make up questions and then swap with another pair.

Helpful hint!

Try using the bullet point button beside the words on your list. This will make your notes clearer to read, e.g.

- *cacti*
- *desert*
- *spines*
- *protect from heat*

Glossary

cactus (plural cacti) — a desert plant that stores water in its flesh spike-covered stem

capital — the main city of a country or State

chariot racing — a race between horse-drawn wheeled vehicles

commission — to officially arrange for a job or a piece of work to be done

cylinder — a tube-shaped object with circular ends tha can be solid or hollow

earthquake — a violent shaking of the ground caused when moving rocks under the Earth's surface release built-up pressure in the for of shockwaves

emperor — a ruler of great power who rules an empire

geologist — a person who studies the layers of rock tha form the Earth

hurricane — a violent storm with a very strong wind

magma — a layer of hot melted rock beneath the soli surface of the earth

Middle Ages — the period of history between about AD 1000 and AD 1500

igrate	to move regularly from one part of the world to another
ummy	a dead body that has been preserved
yxomatosis	a highly infectious and usually fatal disease affecting rabbits
ilgrims	someone who travels a long distance to a holy place
oman Empire	a group of countries under the authority of Rome from 27 BC until AD 395
culpture	a figure, animal, or shape in clay, bronze, marble and so on
lave market	a place where people who are the property of another person and work without pay or rights are sold
tall	a stand, bench or table used to display goods for sale
ornado	a column of fast moving air
olcano	a mountain with an opening at the top through which lava, hot gases and ashes are forced when it erupts

Index